Audience

Reading Level: Grade 4
Interest Level: Grades 3–6
Common Core K–5: RI, RF

Features

24 pages, 8 x 9.5 inches
Reinforced library binding
Full-color photographs and illustrations
Author/Illustrator biography
Index
Infographics
Informative sidebars
Phonetic glossary
Sources for further research
Suggested websites
Table of contents

Actual Font & Size

artifacts show

Titles & Prices

Each Book: $28.50 List / **$19.95 Library**

Complete 8-Book Set: $228.00 List / **$159.60 Library SAVE $68.40!**

Titles & Prices	DWY	ATOS	GRL	LXL	ISBN
					978-15038-13137
★ Crystals, Carla Mooney ©2017	548	–	TBD	610L	978-15038-07990
★ Fossils, Carla Mooney ©2017	560	–	TBD	620L	978-15038-08003
★ Igneous Rocks, M. J. York ©2017	551	–	TBD	610L	978-15038-08010
★ Metamorphic Rocks, Cecilia Pinto McCarthy ©2017	551	–	TBD	590L	978-15038-08027
★ Minerals, Roberta Baxter ©2017	549	–	TBD	610L	978-15038-08034
★ The Rock Cycle, Pam Watts ©2017	551	–	TBD	660L	978-15038-08041
★ Sedimentary Rocks, Roberta Baxter ©2017	551	–	TBD	650L	978-15038-08058
★ Soil, Pam Watts ©2017	630	–	TBD	570L	978-15038-08065

★ NEW FOR FALL 2016

C. World Fall '16 pg 44

FOSSILS

BY CARLA MOONEY

Published by The Child's World®
1980 Lookout Drive • Mankato, MN 56003-1705
800-599-READ • www.childsworld.com

Acknowledgments
The Child's World®: Mary Swensen, Publishing Director
Red Line Editorial: Editorial direction and production
The Design Lab: Design

Design Element: Shutterstock Images
Photographs ©: Shutterstock Images, cover (top), cover
(bottom left), 1 (top), 15, 18; Marcel Clemens/Shutterstock
Images, cover (bottom right), 1 (bottom), 4; iStockphoto,
5, 9, 13, 14; Arpad Benedek/iStockphoto, 7; Linda Epstein/
iStockphoto, 8; Anton Ivanov/Shutterstock Images, 11;
Zack Frank/Shutterstock Images, 12, 23; Marcio Silva/
iStockphoto, 16; Louie Psihoyos/Corbis, 20

ISBN 9781503808003
LCCN 2015958130

Printed in the United States of America
Mankato, MN
June, 2016
PA02305

ABOUT THE AUTHOR

Carla Mooney is the author of many books for young readers. She loves reading and learning about nature's fascinating creations. A graduate of the University of Pennsylvania, she lives in Pittsburgh, Pennsylvania, with her husband and three children.

CONTENTS

CHAPTER 1

What Is a Fossil?

Fossils are from plants and animals that lived long ago. A fossil is the **remains** of a living thing. It is at least 10,000 years old. Some fossils are **preserved** in great detail. Others are not. They contain only traces of a living thing. People often find fossils in rocks. Many are buried beneath Earth's surface. In fact, *fossil* comes from a Latin word meaning "dug up."

A rock contains a dragonfly fossil.

A trace fossil shows dinosaur prints.

Many people know about dinosaur fossils. They have seen dinosaur bones in museums. Old bones are just one type of fossil. There are many other types. Scientists called paleontologists study fossils. They group fossils into two major categories: body fossils and trace fossils.

Body fossils preserve plant or animal body parts. This type of fossil helps show what an animal or plant looked like. Bones, teeth, and shells are body fossils. Leaves, petals, and stems are also body fossils. Sometimes fossils preserve an entire animal or plant. For example, scientists might find a mammoth encased in ice.

Trace fossils are remains of an animal's activities. This type of fossil shows how an animal lived. Animal tracks and footprints are trace fossils. Eggshells and nests are also trace fossils. The trail a worm leaves in the dirt is another type of trace fossil.

Finding a fossil's age can be tricky. Paleontologists use several methods. One is radiometric dating tests. These tests estimate the age of rocks near the fossil. Inside the rocks, some **elements** are radioactive. The radioactive elements fall apart over time. They change into different elements. Scientists measure the radioactive and non-radioactive elements in the rock. This allows them to estimate how old the rock is.

Relative dating is another method. One type of relative dating is stratigraphy. Rocks are formed in layers called strata. The oldest layers are on the bottom. The most recent layers are near the top. A fossil in a bottom layer is probably older than a fossil in a top layer.

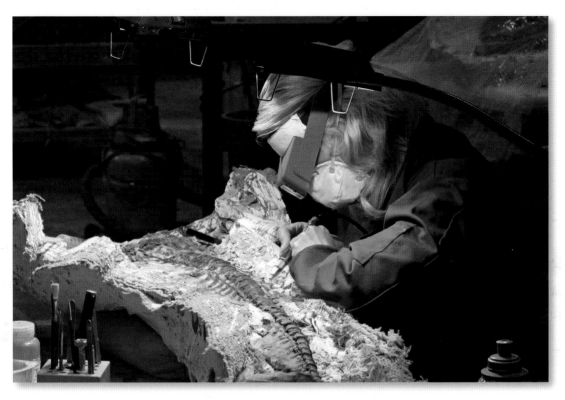

A scientist uses special equipment to study a fossil.

Index fossils can help show a fossil's age. They are from organisms that lived for only a short time. Scientists know when the organisms lived. They can use their fossils to date other fossils. Some fossils are found in the same layer of rock as an index fossil. These fossils are likely near the same age as the index fossil.

CHAPTER 2

How Do Fossils Form?

When a living thing dies, its remains usually **decay**. Over time, they disappear. But sometimes, the remains are buried. Sand, soil, or mud protects them from decay. If conditions are right, these remains become fossils.

Many fossils form when remains are buried in **sediment**. Sediment protects the remains. The sea floor is one of the best places for fossils to form. Mud, sand, and sediment cover the remains.

Most fossils form in layers of sedimentary rock.

Animal or plant remains settle into the sediment. The animal or plant's soft tissue decays. After a while, only its hard pieces are left. The hard pieces include bones and shells. Over time, many layers of sediment bury the remains. The remains are buried deeper and deeper under Earth's surface. Top layers press down on the sediment. This pressure **compresses** the sediment around the remains. The sediment slowly turns into rock.

Sometimes, water carries dissolved **minerals**. The water seeps into the buried remains. Then, the water evaporates. The dissolved minerals form crystals. Pressure causes the remains to harden. This type of fossil is a petrified fossil. *Petrified* means "changed into stone."

Other times, the remains dissolve completely. They leave a hollow space in the rock. The space is in the shape of the bone or shell. This hollow space is called a natural

Petrified wood forms when dissolved minerals crystallize around part of a tree.

FOSSIL FORMATION

A fossil is formed through several steps:

An animal or plant dies. It falls to the ground or into a lake.

↓

The remains break down. Many parts decay or disintegrate.

↓

Layers of sediment cover the remaining parts. These layers harden into rock.

↓

Over time, the rock erodes.

↓

The fossil is exposed on Earth's surface.

mold. Sometimes, water fills the mold. It carries mineral deposits. These mineral deposits form a **cast** of the mold.

CARBONIZATION

Some fossils are formed through carbonization. Animal or plant remains are buried in sediment. Heat and pressure cause the remains to release hydrogen and oxygen. These elements leave behind a residue of carbon. The residue leaves a mark or imprint in the sedimentary rock.

Other times, the mold stays hollow. Paleontologists pour materials inside the mold. Then they make a cast of the fossil.

Sometimes, an animal's entire body is fossilized. Some whole-body fossils are preserved in tar. Others are formed when an animal's body is frozen in ice. This type of fossil preserves the entire body and tissues. The fossil may be preserved for thousands of years. In 2013, scientists discovered the body of a woolly mammoth. It was frozen in ice in Siberia, Russia. The scientists estimate that the animal lived 40,000 years ago.

After a fossil forms, **erosion** can uncover it. Over thousands of years, wind wears away the rock. Bits of rock are carried away. Eventually, the fossil is exposed. Scientists find it on the land surface. Other times, scientists **excavate** and search for fossils.

A mammoth skeleton is on display at the American Museum of Natural History in New York.

CHAPTER 3

Finding Fossils

People discover fossils all over the world. Many are found in Earth's **crust**. The crust is made of three main types of rocks: igneous, sedimentary, and metamorphic.

Igneous rocks form from hot melted rock called magma. As magma rises through the crust, it cools. The magma hardens into igneous rock. Metamorphic rocks form under Earth's surface. Heat and pressure squeeze and fold the rocks. As a result, these rocks often have ribbon-like layers.

Part of a fossilized dinosaur skull was found in Colorado.

Sedimentary rock forms from sediment. The sediment can include particles of sand, shells, and other material. They pile up in layers. Then, the layers harden into rock. Sedimentary rock is usually soft. It may break or crumble easily. Limestone is one type of sedimentary rock.

Most fossils are found in sedimentary rock. The Morrison formation is a sedimentary rock layer in the western United States. It holds many dinosaur fossils. Stegosaurus and allosaurus fossils have been found in the formation.

Fossils can be preserved in other materials. Some animals are preserved in ice. Others are caught in amber. Amber is hardened tree resin. Insects and small

Amber preserves the body of a very old beetle.

In 1956, scientists discovered stromatolites, very old fossils, at Shark Bay in Australia.

THE WORLD'S OLDEST FOSSILS

The oldest known fossils are from cyanobacteria. This is a type of ancient bacteria. The fossils are called stromatolites. Prehistoric sponges are the oldest animal fossils. The sponge fossils were found in western Asia and Australia.

animals can get trapped in sticky resin. When the resin hardens, it becomes amber. The amber preserves the body.

Other fossils have been found trapped in tar. Long ago, animals got stuck in the tar and died. The gooey tar preserved their remains. The

Fossils are often found at the La Brea Tar Pits in California.

La Brea Tar Pits are located in Los Angeles, California. Scientists have found millions of bones trapped there. They have found fossils of ancient mammoths, mastodons, and bison. These animals lived 10,000 to 40,000 years ago.

CHAPTER 4

Studying Fossils

Fossils are records of life on Earth. Scientists study fossils for a few reasons. One is to learn about animals and plants. Another is to learn how Earth has changed.

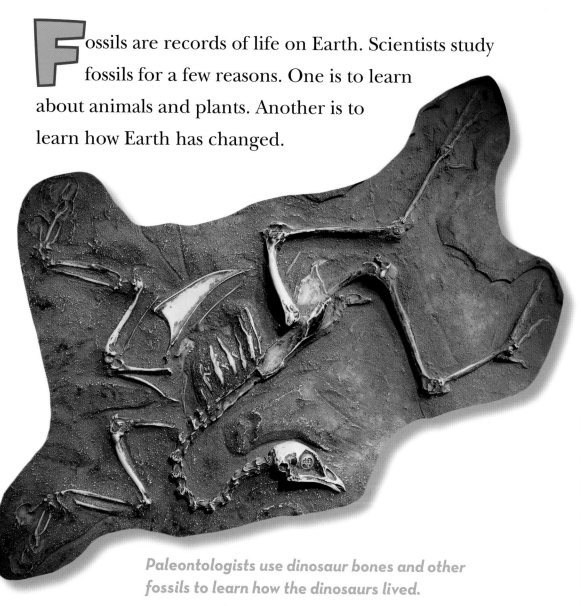

Paleontologists use dinosaur bones and other fossils to learn how the dinosaurs lived.

Paleontologists study many different types of fossils. They study fossils of tiny bacteria. They also study fossils of large animals, like dinosaurs. Some fossils are only a few thousand years old. Others are more than three billion years old.

Paleontologists learn many things from fossils. Fossil bones show what an animal looked like. Using the bones, scientists recreate dinosaur skeletons. These models show how big the dinosaurs were. They can also give clues about how the dinosaurs moved.

Some fossils show how animals behaved. A hadrosaur is a type of dinosaur. Paleontologists have found fossils of many hadrosaurs together. At one site, they found about 10,000 skeletons. Because of this, scientists think that hadrosaurs lived in large herds.

Fossils can give clues about the past. An oyster

DINO DUNG

Ancient dung is one type of trace fossil. The dung shows how the dinosaurs lived. Fossilized waste materials are called coprolites. Scientist William Buckland found the first coprolite in 1823. Recently, paleontologists have studied coprolites to learn what dinosaurs ate. They examine coprolites for plant material or bones. The material shows if the dinosaur ate meat, plants, or both.

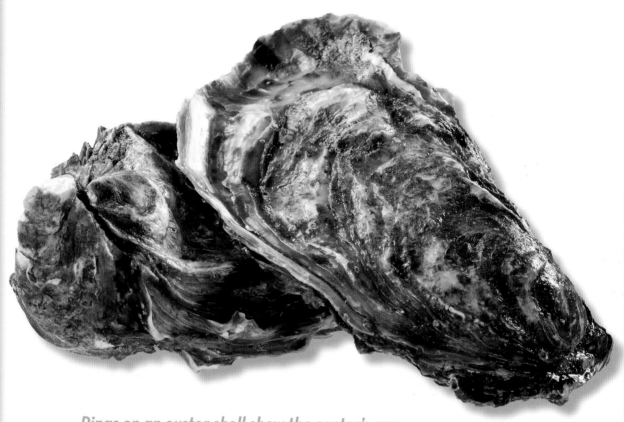

Rings on an oyster shell show the oyster's age.

shell is lined with rings for each year of the oyster's life. Studying the rings tells scientists how long the oyster lived. The rings also tell about the oyster's environment. In good conditions, an oyster grows quickly. It develops thick rings on its shell. If the environment is too hot or too cold, the oyster does not grow as quickly. The rings on its shell are thinner.

Scientists learn about **evolution** from fossils. Fossils give traces of extinct land animals that might be related to whales. They have limbs that are like legs. The limbs are similar to modern whale fins. Scientists believe modern whales evolved from these animals.

Fossils give clues about changes to the **climate**. Paleontologists study plant fossils to learn about the past climate. Plants in warm, wet climates often have thick leaves. Scientists look for clues such as leaf shape and size. These clues tell them about past temperatures and conditions.

Scientists collect fossils in the field. They can work in a wide variety of places. Fossils can be found at the top of a mountain or the bottom of a quarry. The location of a fossil gives scientists important information. It can help them find out when and how the animal or plant died.

Paleontologists use many tools. They use electron microscopes to study the tiniest fossils. X-ray machines help them see inside fossils. Scientists use CT scanners, too. These tools create 3-D models of fossils.

In 2007, paleontologists used a CT scan to study a mammoth. They had found its frozen body in Siberia. They built a 3-D model of its bones and tissue. Mud was

Paleontologists at the British Museum in London arrange dinosaur bones.

in the mammoth's lungs and trunk. They think that the animal died in a muddy river or lake.

Using computer programs, paleontologists analyze fossils. They study plant fossils closely. They also use

COMMON PALEONTOLOGIST TOOLS

Tool	Purpose
rock pick	digging and breaking apart rock
chisel	chipping away rock
dust brush	cleaning fossils
magnifying glass	examining fossils and rock surfaces

computers to create pictures of animals. They rebuild skeletons. Their pictures help them understand the animals' bodies.

Extinct plants and animals are gone forever. But we can still learn about them. Fossils tell us about these lost species. They preserve information about plants and animals. Fossils also help us learn about Earth.

GLOSSARY

cast (*KAST*) A cast is an object that captures the form and shape of another object. Scientists might use a cast to capture the shape of a fossil.

climate (*KLYE-mit*) Climate is the usual weather in a place. Fossils can give clues about an area's past climate.

compresses (*kuhm-PRESS-iz*) When something presses or squeezes an object, it compresses the object. Pressure from layers of rock above compresses sediment beneath Earth's surface.

crust (*KRUHST*) The crust is the outer layer of Earth. Earth's crust holds many fossils.

decay (*di-KAY*) Decay is the rotting or breaking down of something. Plants decay into the soil.

elements (*EL-uh-muhntz*) Elements are substances that cannot be broken into a simpler substance. Elements such as silicon and iron are found in sedimentary rocks.

erosion (*i-ROH-zhuhn*) During erosion, bits of worn rock are carried away by water or wind. Erosion breaks down rocks into smaller particles.

evolution (*ev-uh-LOO-shuhn*) Evolution is the gradual change of living things over thousands or millions of years. Scientists study fossils to learn about evolution.

excavate (*EKS-kuh-vayt*) To excavate is to find something by removing the dirt or other material that covers it. Scientists often excavate fossils.

minerals (*MIN-ur-uhlz*) Minerals are substances found in nature that are not animals or plants. A rock may contain many minerals.

preserved (*pri-ZURVD*) When something is preserved, it is protected in its original state. A fossil is a preserved record of a past life.

remains (*re-MAYNZ*) Remains are the parts of something that was once alive. Fossils are the preserved remains of animals or plants.

sediment (*SED-uh-muhnt*) Sediment is made of pieces of rocks, sand, and dirt. Many fossils are buried in sediment.

IN THE LIBRARY

Gray, Susan H. *Paleontology: The Study of Prehistoric Life*.
New York: Scholastic, 2012.

Squire, Ann O. *Fossils*. New York: Scholastic, 2012.

Tomecek, Steve. *Dirtmeister's Nitty Gritty Planet Earth:
All about Rocks, Minerals, Fossils, Earthquakes, Volcanoes and
Even Dirt*. Washington, DC: National Geographic, 2015.

ON THE WEB

Visit our Web site for links about fossils: **childsworld.com/links**

*Note to Parents, Teachers, and Librarians: We routinely verify our Web links to make
sure they are safe and active sites. So encourage your readers to check them out!*

INDEX